Contents

Introduction

Learning to read is one of the most important skills that children will develop over the next few years. For most children, learning to read and write is a developmental stage similar to learning to walk and talk; they have an innate ability to interpret signs and symbols – the essence of literacy. These very young learners have already been developing the skills necessary to enjoy reading, such as listening to environmental sounds, instrumental sounds, and the sounds of the body. They will be familiar with the sounds of speech, rhythm, rhyme, and alliteration, and already enjoy listening to their favorite stories over and over again.

Literacy Books 1–3 provide valuable tools for learning sound-letter relationships. In order to become skilled, fluent readers, children will need to understand these relationships to gain a comprehensive grasp of phonics. This begins with developing phonological and phonemic awareness, then consistent, explicit, and systemic phonics instruction. Phonological awareness is the ability to identify that spoken language is made up of smaller parts; sentences are made up of words and words are made up of syllables. The next stage is phonemic awareness. This is the ability to identify that syllables can be further broken down into phonemes: the smallest units of sound. Before children can access the sound-letter relationships necessary to decode written words, they must understand that words (whether written or spoken) are made up of sounds.

Each of the sounds (or phonemes) of English can be represented by certain letter symbols (or graphemes). In English, many sounds can be represented by a number of letter symbols; for example, the sound /k/ can be written as *c*, *k*, *ck*, *ch*, *lk*, or even *qu*. These sound-letter relationships can be compared to an alphabetic code, and the aim of phonics is to equip children with the skills to decode what they can see. In order to learn to read, first children need to recognize the individual sounds, then they learn to synthesize (or blend) them to form words. To learn to write, they need to be able to break (or segment) a word into sounds.

Many education experts believe that the systematic teaching of phonological awareness, as a precursor to phonics instruction, is the key that opens the world of reading to children, and that the earlier this takes place, the better. The acquisition of phonological and phonemic awareness is considered the primary factor determining success in the future development of reading for a child.

Literacy Books 1–3

Over the course of the three Literacy Books, all the core phonemes will be presented and practiced, giving children confidence in their early steps in phonics.

Literacy Book 1 covers all the letters of the English alphabet and focuses on initial letter sounds. Literacy Book 2 works progressively through consonant-vowel-consonant words and some of the most common digraphs, and Literacy Book 3 covers the remaining core sounds in English.

In Literacy Books 2 and 3, children will also begin to encounter common words that appear frequently in English, e.g., *a*, *the*, *my*, *is*, *are*, *it's*, *he's*, *she's*. These are "sight words": words that are not decodable and which need to be taught separately so that children can begin to recognize them by sight.

Top tips for teaching literacy

- Start each lesson with a review of one or more previous letter sounds and words.
- When presenting new letters and words, ensure that every child can see the movement of your lips and tongue and imitate the form. Exaggerate the pronunciation of the sound, without distorting the shape of the mouth.
- A class puppet can be used to lead games and activities. Children can be encouraged to talk to the puppet in order to practice new sounds.
- Children can practice forming the letters in many ways, for example:
  - writing in the air using their index finger, wands, or ribbon sticks
  - drawing the letters in sand
  - creating the letters with modeling clay, wool, or a flashlight against a wall
  - using their bodies on the floor, in small groups
  - tracing over the letters in their books.
- As well as recognizing letters, practice recognizing the sounds within words, asking children to indicate (e.g., by clapping or jumping) when they hear one of their target sounds for the lesson. By pointing to your ear and saying a sound, you can clearly show the children that you are referring to a sound, rather than a word.
- If there are any children in the class whose name begins with or contains the target sound, say their names while emphasizing the sound. This will help to create an emotional and environmental link to the sound.
- From Level 2 onward, include activities to encourage children to begin blending and segmenting simple consonant-vowel-consonant (CVC) words.
- Reinforce learning at home. Be patient, flexible, and enthusiastic.

Games

The Games Bank below contains a selection of games and activities that can be used to consolidate knowledge of the sounds covered in the Literacy Books. They can be used as appropriate with the letters and words that the children have covered up to that stage.

Name of the day

Each day, write the name of one child (it could be the class helper for the day) on the board. Invite the class to identify the first sound of the child's name and think of words beginning with that sound.

Letter boxes

Label two boxes each with a target letter. Provide a selection of picture cards showing words the children have seen in the Literacy Books. Invite them to put those beginning with the target letters into the correct boxes while saying the letters.

Find the sound first

Organize the class into two rows, sitting facing each other with a space in the middle. Give the child at the head of each row a basket (or any container). Place a selection of letter cards in the space in the middle of the floor and explain that you are going to say a sound, and the two children holding a basket must race to pick up the correct letter card and put it in their team basket. Once all of the cards have been picked up, and all children have had a turn, count the cards in each basket, encouraging children to say the sounds.

Find your match

Prepare a number of picture cards, making sure that there are at least two different picture cards for each target sound. Hand out the cards to the class and encourage children to find the child whose card features a picture of something that begins with the same sound as their own, for example, the child with the picture of a duck could match with the child with a picture of a doll. Ask the groups to identify the sound they have in common. This game could also be played with rhyming words, or words that end with the same sound.

Musical paper plates

Write letters on paper plates and place the plates in a circle. Play some music as the children walk around the circle, then pause the music and say "Stop!" All the children should stand still behind a plate. Ask *Who is behind /f/ for "foot"?* and encourage that child to raise their hand. Ask the class if they can think of any other words beginning with the same sound. Restart the music and continue the game.

Word poster

Write the letter representing a target word in the middle of a large piece of poster paper. Invite children to draw pictures of the words they know beginning with the target sound on the poster.

How many sounds?

Write a familiar word on the board and ask children to count how many letters the word contains. Give each child some building blocks. Say the word, emphasizing the individual sounds, and ask children to build a tower containing as many blocks as there are sounds in the word. Ask children if there are more letters or more sounds in the word. Repeat with other words.

Find the letter

Give each child a simple book. Say a letter and ask children to try to find in their book words that begin with that letter. Write the words and invite the children to circle the first letter and say each word.

Going on a letter hunt

Choose a letter of the day and ask children to try to find the words that begin with this letter in as many places in the classroom or school as they can.

Memory

Prepare six cards with decodable words known to the children. Help children to read the words, then turn them over, facedown on the table. Say a word and invite children to find the corresponding card.

Surprise eggs

Fill plastic eggs with small letter cards which, when arranged, will form a familiar, decodable word. A small picture card giving a clue as to the word can also be included. Invite children to get into pairs and choose a plastic egg. Encourage children to work together to arrange their letter cards into a word, which they should then sound out. You can use envelopes if you don't have plastic eggs.

Missing letters

Organize children into small groups and give each group a basket or container with a number of letters in it (either letter magnets or letter cards). Say a familiar, decodable word and write it on the board, leaving a space for one of the letters; for example, say *hat*, but write "h_t." Ask children to look in their basket to find the missing letter. Alternatively, do not say the word, but invite children to find a letter that will complete it, for example, "h_t" could be either *hat* or *hot*.

The alphabet

1 🔊001 Listen and follow. 2 🔊002 Listen again and trace.

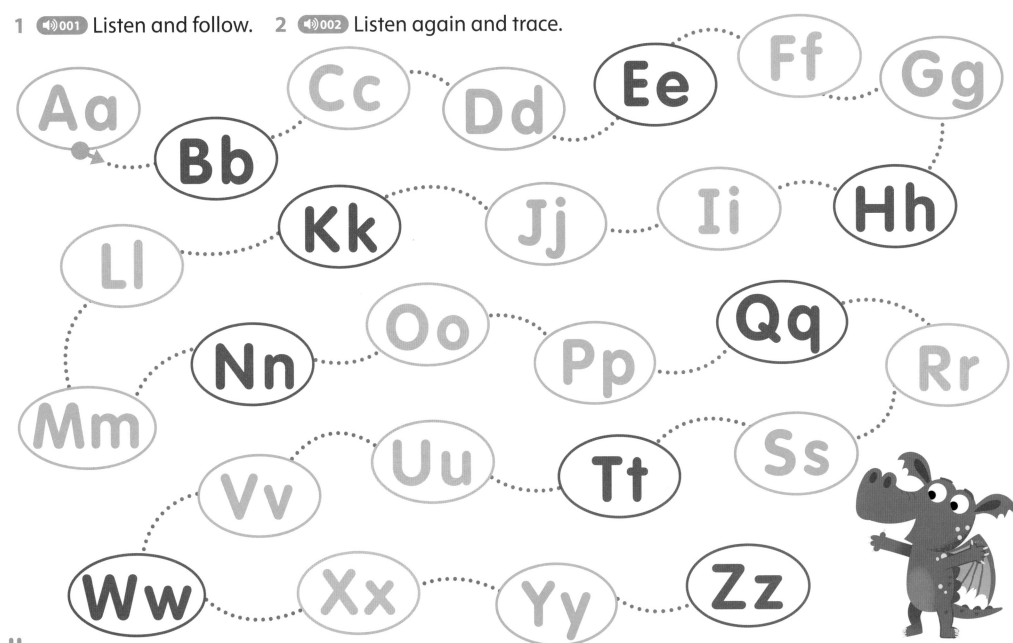

4

1 🔊003 Listen and repeat. Trace.

2 🔊004 Listen, point, and repeat. Find **a** and circle.

apple   **alligator**   **ant**

3 Look and match.

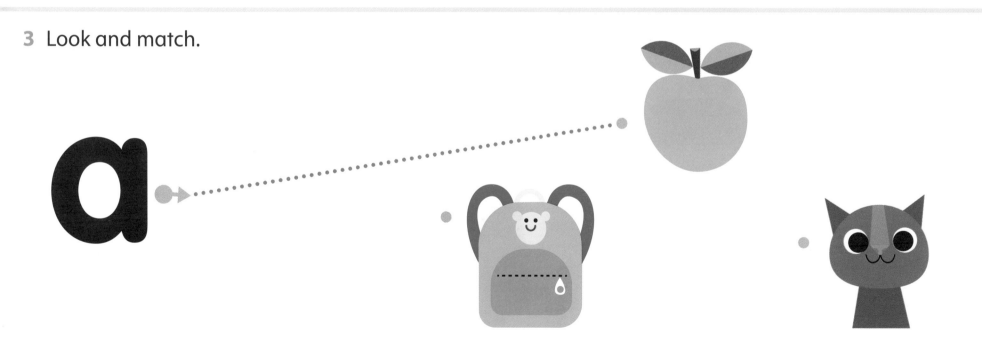

1 🔊005 Listen and repeat. Trace.

2 🔊006 Listen, point, and repeat. Color **b**.

bag   **bed**   **boy**

3 Find **b** and circle.

Language focus: *bag, bed, boy*

1 🔊007 Listen and repeat. Trace.

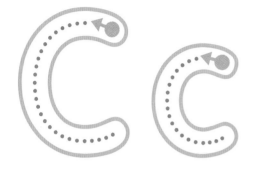

2 🔊008 Listen, point, and repeat. Find **c** and trace.

cat   cup   caterpillar

3 Find **c** and color. What do you see?

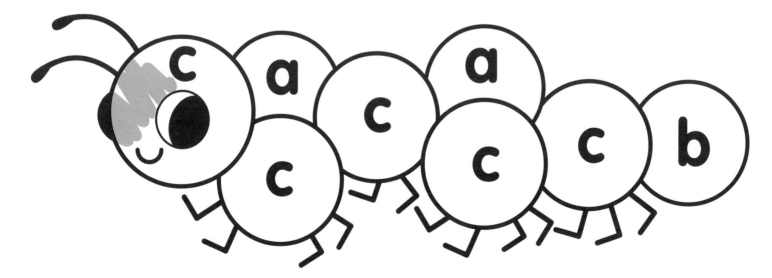

1 🔊 009 Listen, clap, and chant.

A a a an 🍎 and an 🐜

B b b a 🧒 and a 🎒

C c c a ☕ and a 🐱

2 Trace and say.

alligator

bed

caterpillar

3 Trace, say, and match.

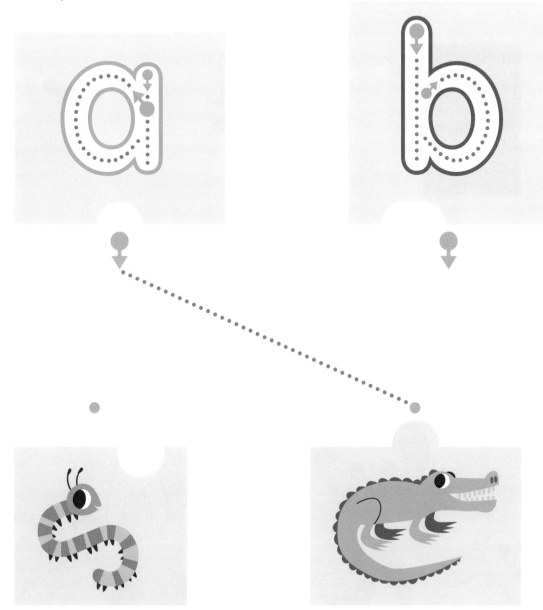

1 🔊010 Listen and repeat. Trace.

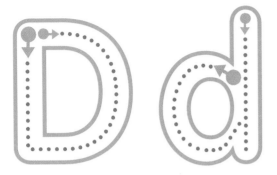

2 🔊011 Listen, point, and repeat. Find **d** and circle.

door　　**doll**　　**duck**

3 Find the **d** words. Color and say.

Language focus: *door, doll, duck*

1 🔊012 Listen and repeat. Trace.

2 🔊013 Listen, point, and repeat. Color **e**.

egg

elbow

elephant

3 Help the baby find the mom.
Follow, trace, and say.

1 🔊014 Listen and repeat. Trace.

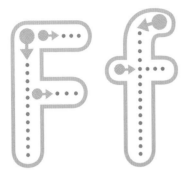

2 🔊015 Listen, point, and repeat. Find **f** and trace.

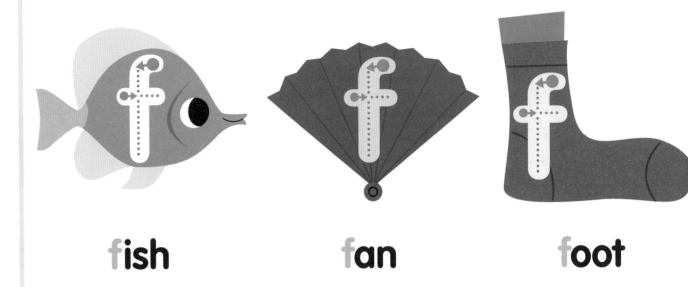

fish   **f**an   **f**oot

3 Find **f** and color.

Language focus: *fish, fan, foot*

1 🔊016 Listen, clap, and chant.

D d d   a   and a

E e e   an   and an

F f f   a   and a

2 Trace and say.

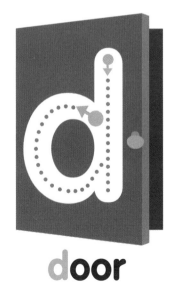

door

elephant

fish

3 Trace, say, and match.

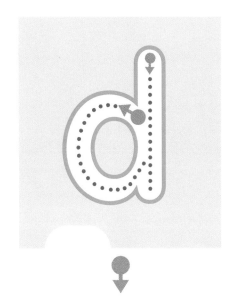

1 (017) Listen and repeat. Trace.

2 (018) Listen, point, and repeat. Find **g** and circle.

game   **goat**   **gift**

3 Find **g** and color.

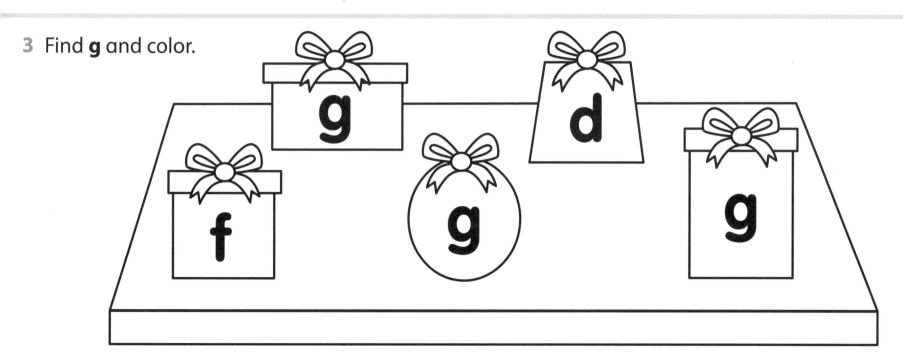

1 🔊019 Listen and repeat. Trace.

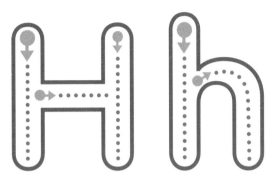

2 🔊020 Listen, point, and repeat. Color **h**.

hoop   **hat**   **house**

3 Find **h** and circle.

1 🔊**021** Listen and repeat. Trace.

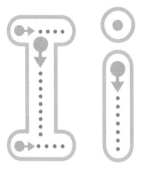

2 🔊**022** Listen, point, and repeat. Find **i** and trace.

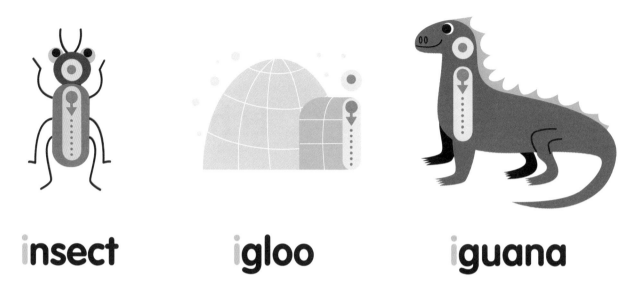

insect   **i**gloo   **i**guana

3 Look and match.

1 🔊023 Listen, clap, and chant.

G g g a   and a

H h h a ⭕ and a 🎩

I i i an 🛖 and an 🪲

2 Trace and say.

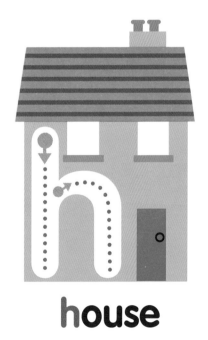

gift   **h**ouse   **i**guana

3 Trace, say, and match.

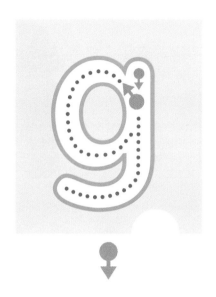

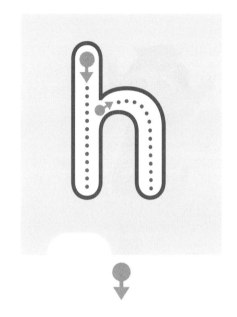

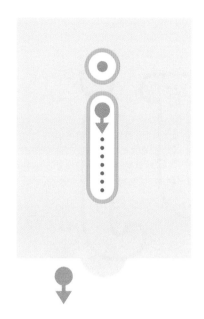

1 🔊024 Listen and repeat. Trace.

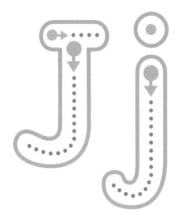

2 🔊025 Listen, point, and repeat. Find **j** and circle.

jump   **jam**   **jacket**

3 Find **j** and circle.

Language focus: *jump, jam, jacket*

1 🔊 026 Listen and repeat. Trace.

2 🔊 027 Listen, point, and repeat. Color **k**.

kite

key

kangaroo

3 Find **k** and color. What do you see?

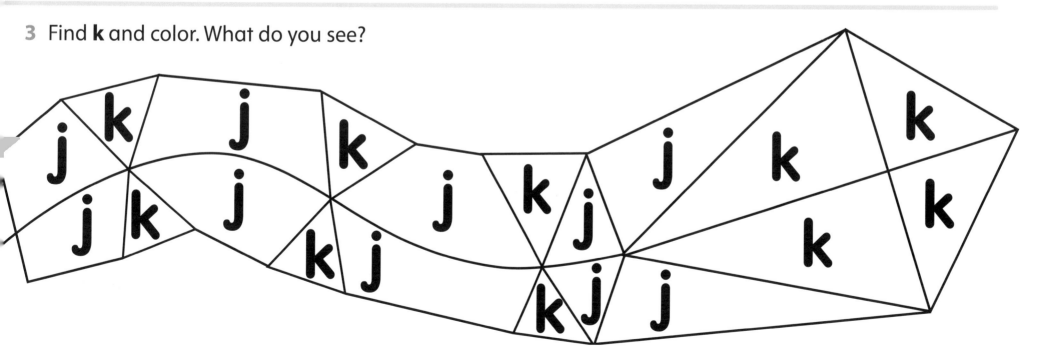

1 🔊 028 Listen and repeat. Trace.

2 🔊 029 Listen, point, and repeat. Find **l** and trace.

leaf　　**l**amp　　**l**emon

3 Find **l** and connect.

1 🔊030 Listen, clap, and chant.

J j j ![boy jumping] and a ![jacket]

K k k a ![kite] and a ![key]

L l l a ![lamp] and a ![lemon]

2 Trace and say.

jam

kangaroo

leaf

3 Trace, say, and match.

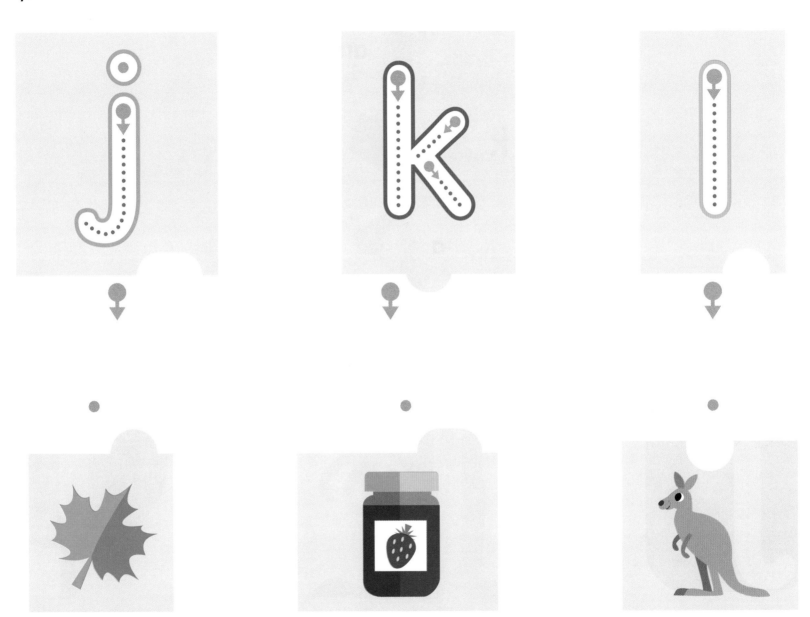

1 🔊 031 Listen and repeat. Trace.

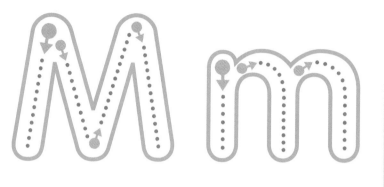

2 🔊 032 Listen, point, and repeat. Find **m** and circle.

mango   **m**op   **m**at

3 Trace, color, and say. What do you see?

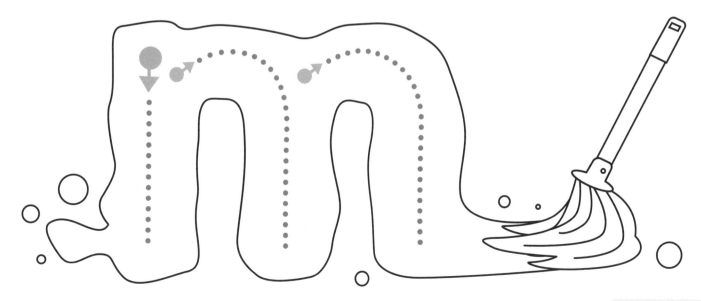

1 🔊033 Listen and repeat. Trace.

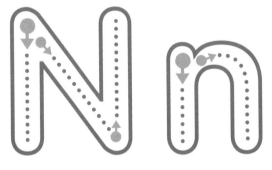

2 🔊034 Listen, point, and repeat. Color **n**.

noodles　　　**nut**　　　**nest**

3 Find **n** and circle.

Language focus: *noodles, nut, nest*

1 🔊035 Listen and repeat. Trace.

2 🔊036 Listen, point, and repeat. Find **o** and trace.

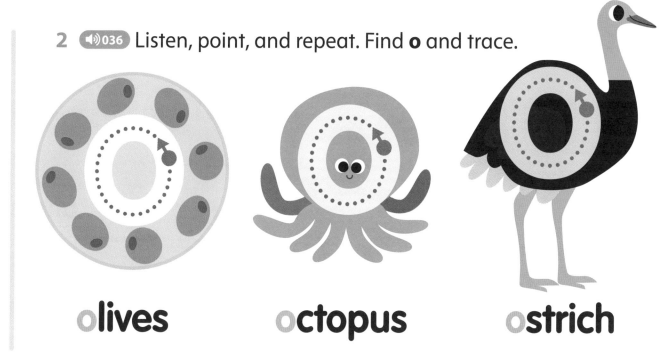

olives   **o**ctopus   **o**strich

3 Look and match.

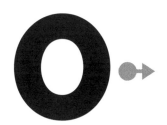

1 🔊 037 Listen, clap, and chant.

M m m   a   🥭   and a   🧹

N n n   🍜   and a   🐦

O o o   🫓   and an   🦤

2 Trace and say.

mat   **nut**   **o**ctopus

3 Trace, say, and match.

 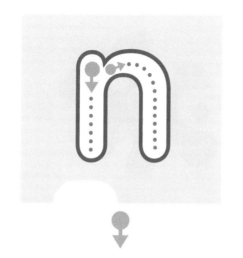 

  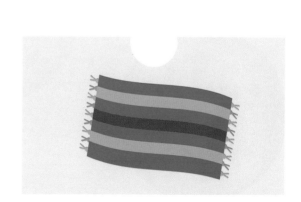

1 🔊038 Listen and repeat. Trace.

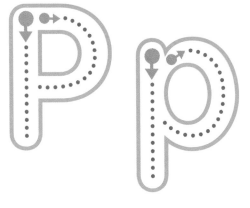

2 🔊039 Listen, point, and repeat. Find **p** and circle.

purple **pet** **pizza**

3 Find **p** and circle.

Language focus: *purple, pet, pizza*

1 🔊040 Listen and repeat. Trace.

2 🔊041 Listen, point, and repeat. Color **q**.

queen   **quilt**   **quail**

3 Find **q** and color.

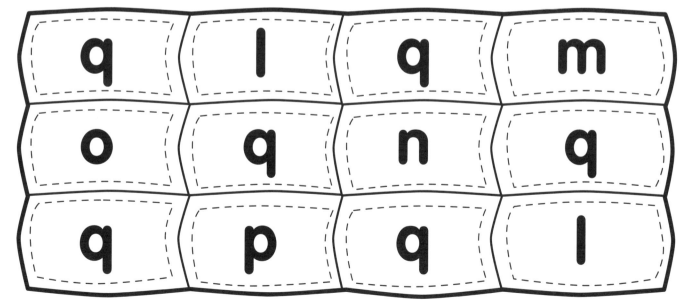

q	l	q	m
o	q	n	q
q	p	q	l

1 🔊042 Listen and repeat. Trace.

2 🔊043 Listen, point, and repeat. Find **r** and trace.

robot　　　**r**ock　　　**r**abbit

3 Find **r** and connect.

Language focus: *robot, rock, rabbit*

1 🔊 044 Listen, clap, and chant.

P p p   a 🍕 and a 🐱

Q q q   a 🐦 and a 👸

R r r   a 🪨 and a 🐰

2 Trace and say.

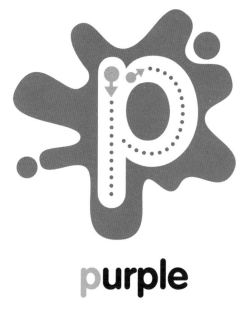

purple

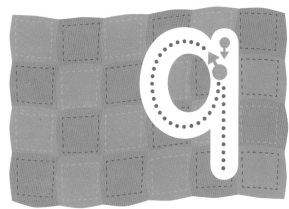

quilt

robot

3 Trace, say, and match.

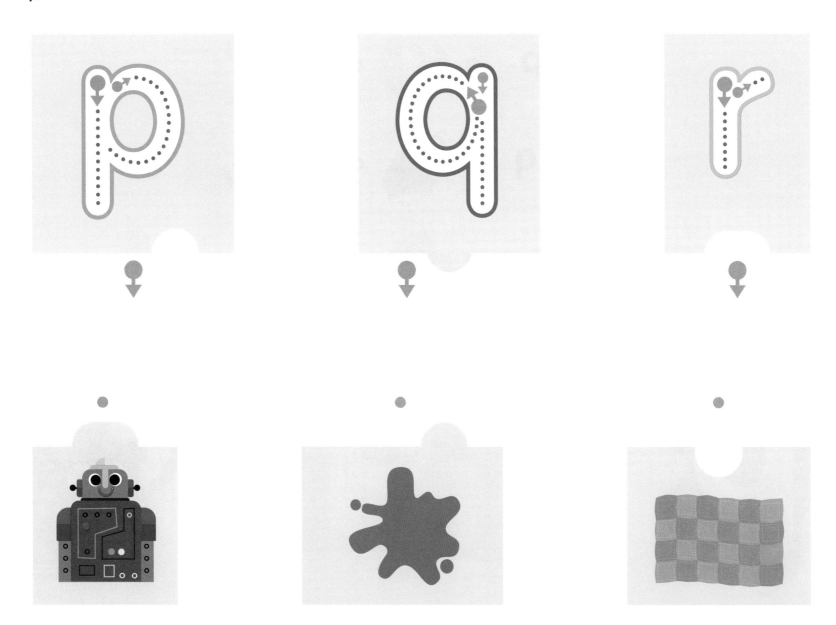

1 🔊045 Listen and repeat. Trace.

2 🔊046 Listen, point, and repeat. Find **s** and circle.

sun   **s**ail   **s**oap

3 Find **s** and color. What do you see?

1 🔊 047 Listen and repeat. Trace.

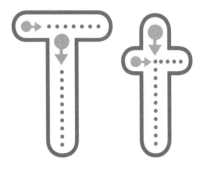

2 🔊 048 Listen, point, and repeat. Color **t**.

turtle **t**able **t**eacher

3 Find the **t** words. Color and say.

1 🔊049 Listen and repeat. Trace.

2 🔊050 Listen, point, and repeat. Find **u** and trace.

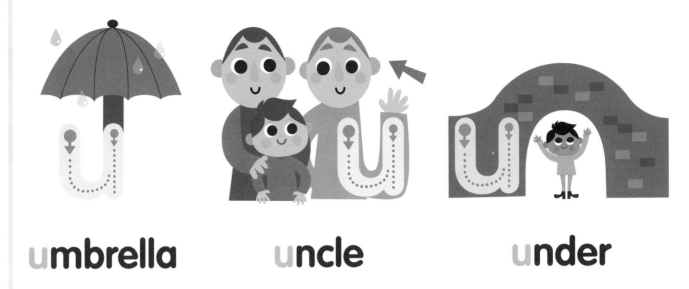

umbrella   **u**ncle   **u**nder

3 Find **u** and circle.

1 🔊051 Listen and repeat. Trace.

2 🔊052 Listen, point, and repeat. Find **v** and trace.

volcano   **van**   **vest**

3 Look and match.

Language focus: *volcano, van, vest*

1 🔊053 Listen, clap, and chant.

S s s   a ☀️ and a ⛵

T t t   a 👩‍🏫 and a 🐢

U u u   🌉 and an 👨‍👦

V v v   a 🦺 and a 🚚

2 Trace and say.

soap

table

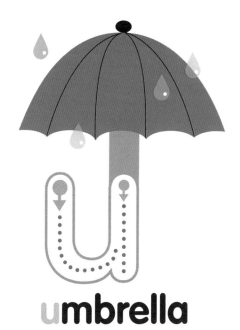

umbrella

volcano

3 Trace, say, and match.

 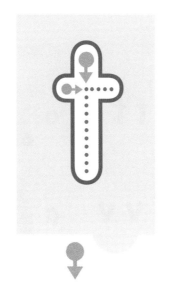  

s t u v Review

1 🔊054 Listen and repeat. Trace.

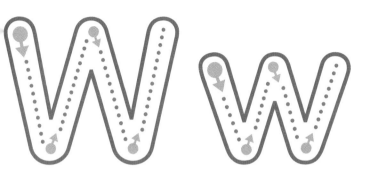

2 🔊055 Listen, point, and repeat. Find **w** and circle.

window　　**web**　　**water**

3 Find **w** and connect.

1 🔊 **056** Listen and repeat. Trace.

2 🔊 **057** Listen, point, and repeat. Color **x**.

box　　　　**fo**x　　　　**a**x

3 Find **x** and circle.

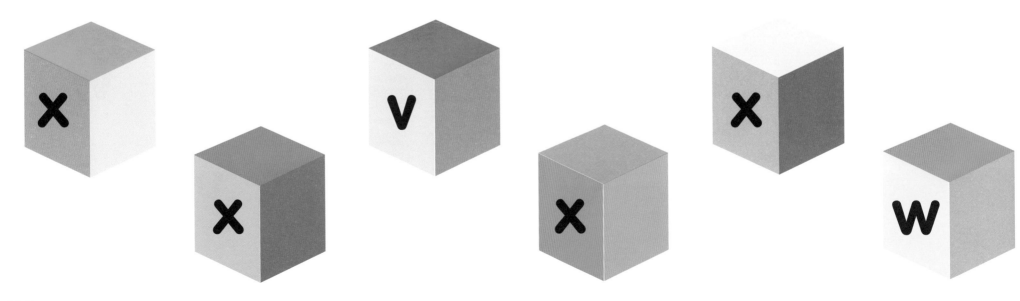

Language focus: *box, fox, ax*

1 ◀))058 Listen and repeat. Trace.

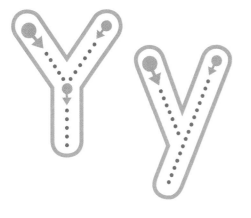

2 ◀))059 Listen, point, and repeat. Find **y** and trace.

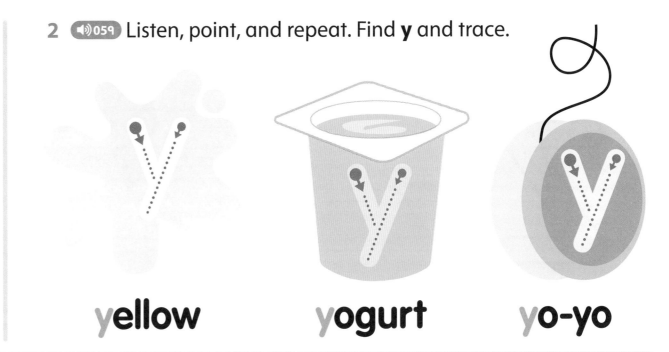

yellow   **yogurt**   **yo-yo**

3 Find **y** and color.

1 🔊060 Listen and repeat. Trace.

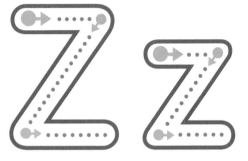

2 🔊061 Listen, point, and repeat. Find **z** and trace.

zebra　　　**zigzag**　　　**zero**

3 Look and match.

Language focus: *zebra, zigzag, zero*

1 🔊062 Listen, clap, and chant.

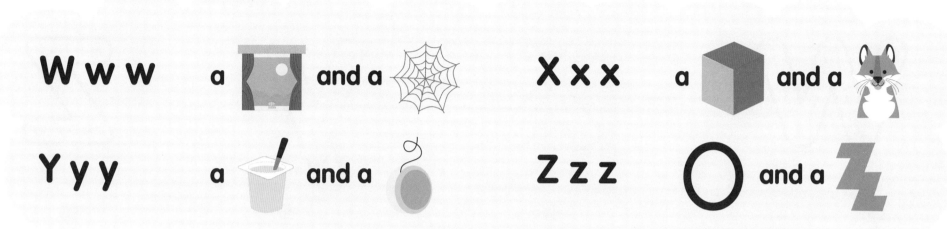

W w w   a [window] and a [web]   X x x   a [box] and a [fox]

Y y y   a [yogurt] and a [yo-yo]   Z z z   O and a [zigzag]

2 Trace and say.

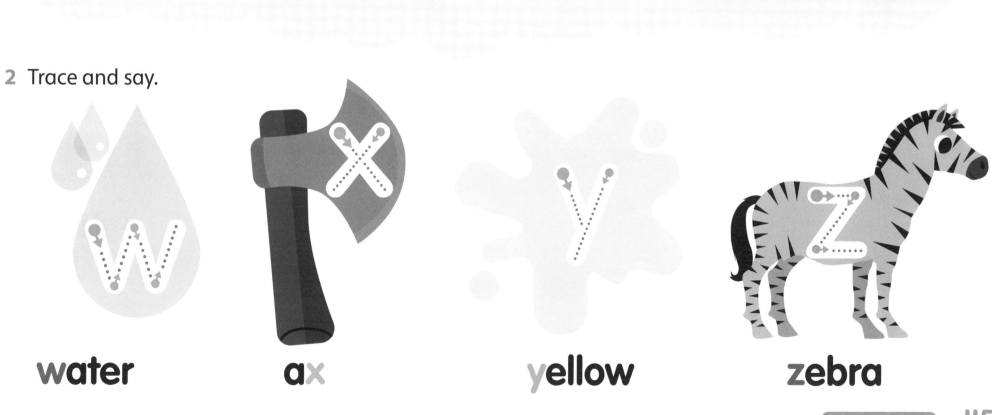

water   a**x**   **y**ellow   **zebra**

3 Trace, say, and match.

I can ...

1 ◀))063 Listen and repeat. Color and say.

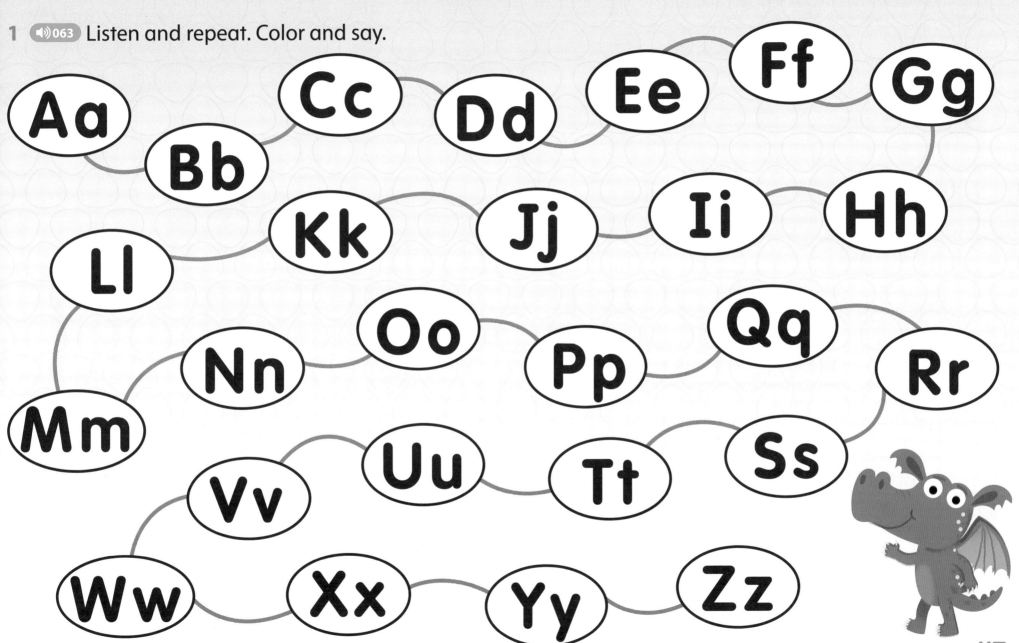

Great Clarendon Street, Oxford, OX2 6DP, United Kingdom

Oxford University Press is a department of the University of Oxford.
It furthers the University's objective of excellence in research, scholarship,
and education by publishing worldwide. Oxford is a registered trade
mark of Oxford University Press in the UK and in certain other countries

ISBN: 978 0 19 486269 1   Little Blue Dot 1 Literacy Book

Printed in China

This book is printed on paper from certified and well-managed sources

ACKNOWLEDGEMENTS

Illustrations by: Sean Sims/Advocate Art. Spark character by Kevin Payne/
Advocate Art. *The publisher would like to thank the following for permission to
reproduce cover photographs:* Shutterstock (artjazz, Avesun, _cz, Kitsana1980,
piyaphon, Vandathai).